The Royal Botanic Gardens, Kew
NATURE JOURNAL

Enjoy the Beauty of the
Natural World

Felicity Forster

The Royal Botanic Gardens, Kew
NATURE JOURNAL

Enjoy the Beauty of the Natural World

SIRIUS

All illustrations included in this book have been taken from the Library, Art & Archives Collections of the Royal Botanic Gardens, Kew.

The views expressed in this work are those of the author and do not necessarily reflect those of the Board of Trustees of the Royal Botanic Gardens, Kew.

This edition published in 2022 by Sirius Publishing, a division of Arcturus Publishing Limited,
26/27 Bickels Yard, 151–153 Bermondsey Street,
London SE1 3HA

ISBN: 978-1-3988-1895-8
AD006692UK

Printed in China

CONTENTS

INTRODUCTION

There's no better feeling than stepping outdoors and experiencing first-hand all that the natural world has to offer – breathing the fresh air, listening to the sound of birds singing in the trees or the wind rustling in the leaves, feeling gentle raindrops on our face or the crunch of footsteps in the snow, appreciating the scent of spring blossom or a muddy woodland walk, looking to the distant horizon or examining a bee landing on a flower. There is so much for us to notice and enjoy.

Research has shown that spending time in nature boosts our mental health and wellbeing, bringing much-needed positivity, happiness and tranquillity into our daily lives. As the environmental philosopher John Muir wrote:

> *'Going to the woods is going home;*
> *for I suppose we came from the woods originally.'*

There are huge benefits in immersing ourselves regularly in the natural world. Being out and about can improve our mood, reduce stress, fear and anger, make us feel more relaxed, lower our blood pressure, improve our physical fitness, boost our immune system, speed up our recovery after an illness, help us feel more confident and even make us live longer. In a very real sense, the power of nature gives value and meaning to our lives.

This journal is a celebration of nature, providing a season-by-season journey throughout the year. It is dotted with practical ideas and projects for you to complete, from pressing flowers and making leaf-print artworks to trying out 'forest bathing' or going for a meditative winter walk, and there both lined and blank pages for you to record your thoughts, poems and ideas as you go along. There are also plant profiles accompanied by beautiful botanical drawings from the archives of the Royal Botanic Gardens, Kew, organized by season to highlight when each can be appreciated at its best.

We hope this book will inspire you to enjoy plants and flowers all year long, and that the natural environment will help to soothe, heal, restore and refresh you, wherever you live.

SPRING

COMMON SNOWDROP
(Galanthus nivalis)

Heralding the first awakenings of new life and seen as a symbol of hope for better times ahead, the common snowdrop is always a welcome sight once the long winter months come to a close. These pretty white flowers grow in gardens, country meadows, woodlands and riversides, and at their most impressive they can form a beautiful carpet of white flowers numbering in their hundreds.

In 1735, Carl Linnaeus named the genus *Galanthus* by combining the Greek word for milk (*gala*) and flower (*anthos*), while the species name *nivalis* is Latin for 'of the snow'. The names are apt because these 'milk flowers of the snow' are white in colour and often seen emerging from the snow. There are around 20 species of snowdrop, all of which are white.

Growing in clumps of nodding flowers with a slightly fragrant scent of honey, snowdrops are hardy perennial bulbs with greenish V-shaped marks on the inner petals and smooth, narrow green leaves. They are very resilient little plants. They colonize readily, either by seed dispersal or by their bulbs dividing spontaneously.

Native to mainland Europe, as well as parts of the Caucasus and Middle East, snowdrops are associated with the Christian festival of Candelmas (2 February). Their white flowers were traditionally used to decorate churches at this time, hence their alternative name of Candelmas Bells.

Galanthus nivalis has also been used medicinally for headaches, as a painkiller and as part of a compound used in the treatment of dementia. It should be noted, however, that the bulbs are poisonous if eaten.

Why not try forest bathing

Wander through a bluebell wood and try the Japanese practice of 'forest bathing'. Turn off your phone, be quiet and calm, relax and breathe in the fresh atmosphere of the woods. Be mindful of your surroundings: look, smell, sense and listen to everything around you. This will reduce your stress levels and boost your health and wellbeing.

JAPANESE FLOWERING CHERRY
(Prunus serrulata)

Cherry blossom is truly an exquisite sign of springtime, with profuse pink flowers suddenly bursting into life on previously bare branches. Although particularly associated with Japan and considered to be Japan's national flower, *Prunus serrulata* is enjoyed all over the world. Many public parks and gardens are designed with row upon row of cherry trees to give maximum impact when they all blossom together.

Also known as the hill cherry, oriental cherry and East Asian cherry, the Japanese flowering cherry is said to symbolize clouds and the transient nature of life. There's nothing so stunning as a clear blue sky punctuated by a blush of delicate new blossoms.

As well as having showy pale pink flowers in early or mid-spring, *Prunus serrulata* has pretty orange and red leaves in autumn and glossy, reddish-brown ornamental bark throughout the year. There are hundreds of cultivars, too, one of the most popular being 'Kanzan', which was developed in the Edo or Tokugawa period (1603–1868) in Japan.

Cherry blossom is often depicted in Japanese woodblock prints, such as Hiroshige's 19th-century series *Thirty-six Views of Mount Fuji* which shows the mountain in varying seasons. In 1912, the tradition of planting Japanese flowering cherry trees in Washington DC originated as a gift from the people of Japan to the United States, and the National Cherry Blossom Festival was designated as an official event in 1935 and continues to the present day, running from late March until early April.

TULIP
(Tulipa greigii)

Tulips are quintessential spring flowers, prized for their showy displays of vibrant colours and interesting shapes. As well carpeting fields in the Netherlands with dazzling swathes of fabulous colour (best seen in April), tulips are often seen naturalized in gardens.

Grown and prized since 1055 in the Tian Shan Mountains, tulips became the symbol of the Ottoman Empire and were later cultivated in Persia. By the 16th century they were introduced into the West, and in 17th-century Europe a period known as 'tulip mania' emerged during the Dutch Golden Age. The price of the bulbs skyrocketed as their popularity increased, and the flowers were immortalized in paintings by Flemish artists such as Jan Breughel the Elder, Ambrosius Bosschaert and Paulus Theodorus van Brussel.

Like many tulip species, *Tulipa greigii* originated from Turkestan in Central Asia. It was first described by the German horticulturalist and botanist Eduard von Regel in 1873, the species name commemorating Samuel Grieg, a Russian naval admiral who was once president of the Russian Horticultural Society.

Tulipa greigii, also known as Greig's tulip or Turkestan tulip, produces bowl-shaped flowers in a range of colours – principally red, yellow and white – and has distinctively spotted or striped green and purple-maroon leaves. The blooms are large in comparison to the plant's height, making the flowers stand out well in rockeries and containers. They are a gardener's delight because the bulbs can be left in the ground for several years, with the flowers returning reliably each spring.

Plant some seeds and watch them grow

Take a pot with a hole in the bottom and fill it with compost. Pour in some water, then gently poke your seeds into the compost. Try sunflowers, sweet peas, nasturtiums, beans or carrots. Remember to write labels to remind you what you've planted. Put your pot on a saucer on a sunny windowsill and water it occasionally.

RHODODENDRON
(Rhododendron dalhousiae)

In 1847, the British botanist Sir Joseph Dalton Hooker explored Sikkim, an Indian state in the eastern Himalayas, and found a rhododendron that he proclaimed to be 'the noblest species of the whole race'. It grows in broad-leaved forests usually as an epiphyte in trees, but also on cliffs, boulders and steep slopes.

Hooker brought specimens back to England. He had happened to travel from England to India on the same ship as the Governor-General of India, the 10th Earl of Dalhousie, and the species was dedicated to the latter's wife, Lady Dalhousie, as *Rhododendron dalhousiae* Hook.f. in 1849. Soon after, Hooker was appointed Assistant-Director of the Royal Botanic Gardens, Kew, and his botanical findings were published and illustrated with lithographs by Walter Hood Fitch.

Rhododendron dalhousiae has garnered attention and awards for its very special qualities. It has large clusters of 11-cm (4-inch) fragrant tubular flowers that can be white, cream or pale yellow, providing a striking contrast to the dark green foliage of the tree on which it grows. Viewed high up in the lofty canopy, it makes a spectacular sight in spring.

There are more than a thousand wild species of rhododendron, mostly found the northern hemisphere. *Rhododendron dalhousiae* grows in mild climates, but can also flourish in containers in harsher conditions.

DOG ROSE
(Rosa canina)

Forever associated with fairy tales and romance, we are all familiar with images of medieval princesses living in castles with wild roses scrambling up the stone walls. Shakespeare mentioned the rose in his works more than any other flower, immortalizing it in lines such as: 'What's in a name? That which we call a rose/By any other name would smell as sweet.' (*Romeo and Juliet*).

Rosa canina, or dog rose, is a wild rose that is native to Europe, northwest Africa and western Asia. Also going by the names of dog berry, witch's briar, bird briar and wild briar, it is a thorny climber that likes entwining itself among hedgerows, woodland edges and on scrubland. The large, open, five-petaled flowers vary in colour, but are usually pale pink or white, and they have a delicate, sweet scent in early summer.

As well as being attractive to wildlife, the dog rose is known for its culinary, medicinal and cosmetic applications. The petals can be made into scented sachets or distilled into rosewater, and its rose hips used to make syrups and oils. In Ancient Greece, *Rosa canina* flowers were used to treat colds and sore throats, while the Romans used an infusion of its petals for flavouring their pastries.

If you need any further evidence of the rose's emotional significance, look no further than the Scottish poet Robert Burns, whose well-loved poem *A Red, Red Rose* (1794) begins: 'O, my Luve is like a red, red rose/That's newly sprung in June.'

At its happiest growing in full sunshine, *Rosa canina* is a quintessential summertime plant. Just be aware of the thorns.

Take an early morning walk and listen to the dawn chorus

The warmest months of the year are the best time to hear songbirds. Choose a fine, clear day with little wind and go for an early-morning walk 30 minutes before sunrise. Listen to the dawn chorus and make notes about any birds, animals and insects that you see or hear.

PURPLE CONEFLOWER
(Echinacea purpurea)

Originating in North American rocky, open woodlands and prairies, *Echinacea purpurea* was one of the most important medicinal plants used by Native Americans, and it remains one of the most popular herbal remedies available today. It is commonly used as a treatment for colds, sore throats, coughs and fevers, as well as for generally boosting the immune system.

The name is derived from the Greek *echinos* (hedgehog) and *purpurea* (purple-red) – referring to the petals' spiky shape and bright colour – but the medicinal parts of the plant are the root stalk and sometimes the juice from the above-ground parts.

Prairie-living Native Americans such as the Cheyenne, Dakota (Sioux and Oglala), Kiowa, Crow, Omaha, Pawnee, Ponca, Teton, Delaware and Comanche used *Echinacea* as a panacea for a wide range of ailments, treating everything from sore gums and burns to snake bites. As early settlers continued the tradition, scientists soon began studying its infection-fighting and wound-healing properties, and confirmed its effectiveness.

Echinacea purpurea was originally named *Rudbeckia purpurea* by Carl Linnaeus in 1753, but it was reclassified and given its own genus by the German botanist Conrad Moench in 1794. An important member of the daisy family, the purple coneflower – also known as Eastern purple coneflower, hedgehog coneflower, black samson or purple daisy – has long-lasting summer blooms, the nectar of which is very attractive to bees, butterflies and hummingbirds. Once the petals fall, birds love to eat the blackened cone-shaped seed heads.

AFRICAN LILY
(Agapanthus africanus)

An elegant, long-stemmed plant with strap-like leaves, agapanthus is prized for its large spheres of lily-like blooms in summer. Its Latin name comes from the Greek *agape* meaning 'love' and *anthos* meaning 'flower', making it the 'flower of love'. Despite its common names of African lily, South African lily, Egyptian lily and lily of the Nile, it is actually only native to South Africa, where it grows on rocky sandstone slopes.

Found by the Dutch East India Company on the Cape of Good Hope, a region rich with unique flora, it was imported to the Netherlands, from where it was popularized around the world. In Australia, African lilies are traditionally planted as a welcoming entrance on either side of a front gate or driveway.

There are many different species of African lily, *africanus* being the large evergreen one (smaller ones come from cooler regions and are deciduous). Their main attraction is their globes of trumpet-shaped flowers standing at the top of architectural, drumstick-like stalks. The best-known flowerheads are deep blue or purple, but they also come in powder-blue, pink and pure white. They grow well in containers, and the amazing strength of their slender stems makes them ideal for use as cut flowers.

Immortalized by the Impressionist artist Claude Monet in several paintings of his garden at Giverny, *Agapanthus* also has a rich history of magical and medicinal uses. Tribes in South Africa used the roots to make necklaces to ensure happiness and fertility; flowers were used for antenatal and postnatal care and to treat a variety of conditions from colds to heart disease.

Why not try making a collage?

Collect some different-coloured petals, leaves, grasses and seeds and put them into a flower press or between two sheets of paper with some weights on top to flatten them. When dry, stick them onto some card or make your own nature collage. Try creating a pretty shape such as a heart.

GIANT WATER LILY
(Victoria amazonica)

The national flower of Guyana and the world's largest water lily, *Victoria amazonica* was named in honour of the young Queen Victoria. It is famous for its enormous floating circular leaves with upturned rims, which can grow up to 3 metres (10 feet) in diameter and are strong enough to support the weight of a small child. The reason for this amazing buoyancy is that the bottoms of the leaves are covered with spines to help support the ribs – a structural quality that inspired Joseph Paxton's design of the iron-and-glass Crystal Palace in London.

Having been discovered in the Amazon basin in the early 19th century and originally named *Victoria regia*, seeds of the giant water lily were brought to the Royal Botanic Gardens, Kew, in 1846. It took a while to produce viable plants, and when it finally happened the public were captivated and beautiful botanical illustrations were made by Walter Hood Fitch and William Jackson Hooker.

As well as the remarkable lily pads, the giant water lily has a submerged stalk up to 8 metres (26 feet) long. This is covered with sharp red spines that deter fish predators. When the white flowers bloom in the summer, they are very short-lived, only lasting two days before they sink down into the water. They open at night, emitting a sweet butterscotch-and-pineapple scent that attracts scarab beetles. Pollination is achieved by the petals closing over the beetle, trapping it for a day and coating it in pollen, then the flower – which becomes pinky-purple – opens the next night to release the beetle and allow it to transfer the pollen to a different flower.

AUTUMN

JAPANESE MAPLE
(Acer palmatum)

A very popular deciduous shrub or small tree, *Acer palmatum* produces a spectacular display of red, purple, bronze, yellow or orange leaves in autumn. The leaves are jagged with five, seven or nine lobes, hence the species name *palmatum*, which means 'in the shape of a hand'.

Known by its common names of Japanese maple, palmate maple or smooth Japanese maple, *Acer palmatum* is native to Japan and Korea, but it is most associated with Japan, having been cultivated there for many centuries. The first recorded plant dates as far back as the 7th century, and more than a thousand cultivars have been developed since then.

Acer palmatum was introduced to Europe by the Swedish botanist Carl Peter Thunberg, who had studied under Carl Linnaeus at Uppsala University and later became known as the 'Japanese Linnaeus'. In the late 1700s, Thunberg spent time in Japan and gave the tree its Latin name. He returned with detailed drawings of *Acer palmatum*, and the species soon became an essential focal point in every oriental-style garden.

There is considerable variation in *Acer palmatum* cultivars. Some have feathery yellow foliage such as 'Koto-no-ito'; some have vibrant red star-shaped leaves such as 'Twombly's Red Sentinel'; and some have rich purple leaves such as 'Bloodgood'. *Acer palmatum* has also become iconic as a bonsai tree. In fact, it is said that no bonsai collection is complete without a Japanese maple.

Make a leaf-print artwork

Gather a selection of fallen autumn leaves: large, small, different shapes and sizes. Place each leaf on some scrap paper with the veins facing upwards. Paint the surface of the leaf, then turn it paint side down and press it onto some paper. Repeat the process using different colours and leaves until you are happy with your multi-coloured design.

ROCK SPRAY COTONEASTER
(Cotoneaster horizontalis)

In the autumn, the deciduous shrub *Cotoneaster horizontalis* doubles its rewards: not only does it burst with a profusion of bright red berries after a blush of small pinkish-white flowers, but the glossy dark green leaves also turn a stunning orange-red before they fall. A third attraction is the pretty herringbone structure of the branches, making the shrub ideal for growing against a wall or as ground cover in a sunny border.

Rock spray cotoneaster, also known as wall spray, rock cotoneaster and wall cotoneaster, is a member of the rose family (Rosaceae), closely related to hawthorn and firethorn. It is native to temperate areas in China and neighbouring countries, where it grows on rocky, mountainous slopes that are exposed to a lot of sunlight. It was introduced to Europe, North America, Australia and New Zealand because of the abundance and beauty of its autumn berries, which persist into winter.

Bees, birds (especially blackbirds and thrushes), butterflies and other pollinators are attracted to the tiny, nectar-rich flowers, and when included as part of a wildlife hedge, it provides shelter and habitat for small mammals, insects and spiders.

Although enjoyed as a popular ornamental plant around the world, it should be noted that rock spray cotoneaster has been so successful that it is now considered an invasive weed if allowed to naturalize in the countryside. For this reason, *Cotoneaster horizontalis* needs to be carefully controlled in gardens.

MAIDENHAIR TREE
(Ginkgo biloba)

Dating back some 200 million years, the maidenhair tree is one of the oldest living tree species in the world. It has existed since before the time of the dinosaurs, and has remained essentially unchanged since then, hence its alternative name of fossil tree.

The maidenhair tree occupies a unique place in botany. Most flowering plants consist of hundreds of thousands of living species and their relatives, but *Ginkgo biloba* is a single, solitary species with no relatives. Every other plant in the Ginkgophyta division is extinct.

Ginkgo biloba is native to China, and it is said that Confucius gave his teachings while sitting under a maidenhair tree. Now, only a few populations remain in its wild habitat and the species has become one of the most threatened on the planet.

The trees are large and grow slowly to a height of up to 35 metres (115 feet). The overall shape is irregular with a spreading crown and the leaves have a distinctive, exotic fan shape with two lobes (*biloba* means two-lobed). Disagreeably scented yellow fruits are borne on female trees, each containing a single large seed.

The best time to appreciate the tree is in autumn, when the leaves turn a stunning bright golden-yellow. The leaves fall quickly, but *Ginkgo biloba* is extremely long-lived, the oldest known example being an incredible 3,500 years old. Kew is home to a specimen that was planted in 1762. It is one of Kew's five 'Old Lion' trees (ancient trees with known dates) and one of the oldest and most revered ginkgos in Europe.

Write a poem inspired by nature

You might think about your favourite tree, place or activity. What do you love most about it, and why? Think about what the place looks like, how it smells and what sounds you can hear, and incorporate your feelings and emotions into your writing.

NERINE
(Nerine bowdenii)

Just when everything else in the garden is dying back and getting ready for winter dormancy, *Nerine bowdenii* comes into its own with a late display of rich pink flowers. Nerines are South African bulbs which, unlike many other bulbs, flower in the autumn. They belong to the family Amaryllidaceae and produce sprays of narrow, lily-like blooms in curly funnel shapes on tall, leafless stems.

The genus name *Nerine* comes from Nereids, sea nymphs in ancient Greek mythology who were said to symbolize beauty and kindness. They accompanied Poseidon, the god of the sea, and helped the Argonaut sailors in their quest to find the Golden Fleece. The species name *bowdenii* commemorates Athelstan Cornish-Bowden, the South African land surveyor who shipped some nerine bulbs to his mother in Devon, England, in 1902. She then sent them on to the Herbarium at Kew Gardens, and two years later they received their scientific name.

Despite not being a true lily or originating in Cornwall or the Channel Islands, common names for *Nerine bowdenii* include Cornish lily, Cape flower, Bowden lily and Guernsey lily. This last name is also applied to *Nerine sarniensis*, one of 25–30 related species. According to legend, nerine bulbs from a 17th-century shipwreck washed up on Guernsey's shore and naturalized among the sand dunes in 1659.

Because the blooms appear after the leaves have died back, the plants have an architectural, upright structure. Their hardiness and prolonged flowering time make them a fabulous plant to enjoy in the autumn, with cut flowers lasting well into winter.

WINTER

DOGWOOD
(Cornus alba)

Typically grown for its vibrant winter colour, *Cornus alba* is a deciduous shrub that puts on a spectacular display of slender coral-red stems after its leaves have fallen away. The stunning colour of *alba* is the brightest of all the *Cornus* species and looks positively dazzling when the plant catches the sun in a bare winter garden.

Cornus alba is native to Siberia, north China and Korea, and its common names include red-barked, white, Siberian or Tatarian dogwood. There are many cultivars, one of the most popular being *Cornus alba* 'Sibirica', which has crimson stems, white-margined leaves, creamy white flowers and clusters of white berries.

Growing up to 3 metres (10 feet) high, the tall, wiry red stems of dogwood add startling drama to winter gardens. Because the wood is so hard, *Cornus alba* has been important historically. It has been used for making all manner of sharp objects, such as daggers, skewers and arrows, and it was believed that it produced the best charcoal for gunpowder.

The name *Cornus* is Latin for 'horn', likely referring to the hardness of the wood, and there are two theories explaining the origins of the common name. The first is that it was derived from *dagge*, meaning 'dagger' in Old English, and the second is that the bark was once used to wash mangy dogs. By the 16th century, the name 'dog-tree' took over, and from there it evolved into 'dogwood'.

In the 18th century, American pioneers used dogwood twigs to brush their teeth, and *Cornus* timber has been used in the manufacture of an enormous range of items that require strong and hard wood.

Feed the birds!

Put some peanuts, seeds, fat balls and
mealworms outside in hanging feeders
or on a bird table, and fill a bird bath
or saucer with fresh water every day.
Experiment with different types of foods
and make notes about who comes to
visit. Which birds like which seeds?

POINSETTIA
(Euphorbia pulcherrima)

Native to Mexico, *Euphorbia pulcherrima* has bright red leafy bracts that open in winter. Their stunning colour makes them popular as houseplants, especially at Christmas in the northern hemisphere. In fact, they are the best-selling potted plant in the United States, with more than 70 million typically sold over the holiday season.

Euphorbia pulcherrima, which means 'the most beautiful Euphorbia', was given its common name in honour of the botanist Joel Roberts Poinsett, the first US Ambassador to Mexico and co-founder of the Smithsonian Institute, who shipped specimens home from Mexico to his greenhouse in South Carolina in 1828. Poinsettia has many other common names, too, including Christmas star, fire-on-the-mountain, fire plant, lobster flower, Mexican Easter flower, Mexican flameleaf and painted leaf.

The Aztecs called it *cuetlaxochitl* (ket-la-sho-she), and an old Mexican legend explains how poinsettias and Christmas first came together. A poor Mexican girl called Pepita is said to have visited a Nativity scene at a chapel but had nothing to give to the baby Jesus. Her cousin reminded her that 'even the most humble gift, given in love, will be acceptable in His eyes', so she gathered some weeds from the roadside and made them into a simple posy. To everyone's surprise, the handful of weeds was miraculously transformed into a beautiful bouquet of crimson *cuetlaxochitl*, and from that day on, the plant became known as *flor de Nochebuena* (Christmas Eve flower).

There are more than 100 varieties of poinsettia available. The red colour dominates, but there are also pink, white, yellow, purple and salmon-coloured cultivars.

WINTER HEATH
(Erica carnea)

Snow, ice and wind do not bother the winter heath. One of about 800 species of heath, *Erica carnea* forms winter mounds of dainty bell-shaped flowers in grasslands, fens and bogs in cool mountains and coniferous woodlands. Although the species name *carnea* means 'flesh pink', the tubular blooms can actually be pink, magenta, purple, red or white, and all have evergreen, needle-like leaves.

Also known as alpine heath, winter-flowering heath, snow heath or spring heath, *Erica carnea* is a dwarf species of heath found in the wild throughout the Alps of central Europe and countries bordering the Adriatic Sea. It belongs to the large family Ericaceae, which includes cranberries, blueberries, huckleberries and rhododendrons, as well as heaths and heathers (heaths are shorter than heathers and have needle-like leaves borne in whorls; heathers are taller and have flat, scale-like leaves).

Grown around the world as an ornamental garden plant – often accompanying dwarf conifers – there are more than 100 cultivars of *Erica carnea*. No matter what the colour, all provide a vital lifeline for bees, butterflies and moths when little else is flowering.

The honey from *Erica carnea* is amber in colour, turning light yellow when crystallized. It smells and tastes like caramel, dried fruit and flowers, and as well as providing food, it can be used medicinally. Winter heath honey is an effective antiseptic that can make wounds heal more quickly, and it can also soothe sore throats, relieve fatigue and is a healthy source of antioxidants.

Erica carnea brings brightness and colour to potentially dull winter gardens, and it is a natural weed suppressant.

Wrap up warm and take a meditative walk on a frosty day

Be mindful of the sensation of walking
and pay attention to all the sounds,
smells and sights around you – the
trees, leaves, flowers, birds and insects,
the wind, rain or snow. Breathe deeply,
inhale the refreshing scent of the
air and clear your mind. Afterwards,
write down as many things as you
can remember about your walk.

EASTERN CYCLAMEN
(Cyclamen coum)

Often seen growing around the base of deciduous trees, *Cyclamen coum* is a small, tuberous perennial that provides a welcome splash of winter colour among the drab browns of the shaded woodland floor. The foliage appears in late autumn in the form of heart-shaped, mottled green leaves that are sometimes adorned with variegated silver patterns, then the delicate, nodding flowers follow in winter, shaped like miniature pinky-purple shells or upturned turbans. The blooms can be so abundant that they almost completely obscure the glossy leaves.

Cyclamens are members of the primrose family, and their qualities were highly praised by the early 20th-century British horticulturalist and writer Edward Augustus Bowles, who wrote that they 'pay good rent' because of their dainty flowers and attractive leaves, and 'I know of no other plant that will turn patches of dust under thick trees into stretches of beauty so permanently and thoroughly.'

Known as eastern cyclamen, eastern sowbread, Persian violet or round-leaved cyclamen, *Cyclamen coum* is one of about 20 species of cyclamen. It is native to woodlands and rocky areas ranging from Bulgaria to Turkey and countries bordering the eastern Mediterranean, especially Israel, Syria and Lebanon, and can tolerate very cold temperatures in the open. The species name *coum* is thought to refer to Koa or Quwê, an ancient region in Cilicia (now southern Turkey).

A hardy little plant, *Cyclamen coum* brightens up the darkest corners of the winter garden, lifts the spirits and is a timely reminder that spring is just around the corner.